THE SOUND OF CONFLICT

Matthew Calber

ISBN:
979-12-200-2392-4

DEDICATION

I dedicate this book to my cousin, who is no longer with us, and to all women who seek love and freedom.

CHAPTERS

ACKNOWLEDGMENTS

Thanks to the women who inspired me and gave me the opportunity to listen to the stories of their lives.

INTRODUCTION

Before you start reading this book, I would like to give you a gift. Let's just say that I would like to give you the opportunity to start the book in a new way, perhaps already known to some, but undoubtedly useful when trying to fully understand some of the concepts I have described on these pages. You have to adopt a receptive approach, one that gives you the mental openness and the kind of tranquillity needed to enjoy the journey.

Follow my advice, you can also use these pointers when reading other books, should you so wish.

Firstly, the most important thing is to exclude any external disturbances, so without further ado turn off, I repeat, turn off any possible source of disturbance, the television, mobile phone, tablet or computer. Make sure that nothing and nobody can disturb your reading time, this is your little space away from the world, enjoy it!

Now, I would kindly ask the ninety percent of you who set their devices to mute, instead of turning them off, to follow my humble advice and turn them off, which means just that, so play fair. That includes you, because I know that even though you have muted the phone and placed it under the pillow, in ten seconds' time you will go and check if there are any messages. I can see you.

Right, now that you're in "do not disturb" mode, or for the more pragmatic, in "I'm relaxing, don't hassle me" mode, you're almost ready to start reading, so here is just a little more helpful advice.

Get comfortable and prepare your favourite drink or snack, which will accompany you when reading. Any drink is fine, even perhaps a good beer, the important thing is that it is of your liking and that it makes you happy. Now, it is imperative that you enter into a state of relaxation and tranquillity, primarily for your own wellbeing, but also to help with your reading.

Close your eyes, relax, take three deep breaths, breathe in, then exhale. As you exhale, as well as air, imagine you are expelling all your worries, all your negative thoughts, everything that is not important at the moment and disturbs your calm. Then, imagine being in a beautiful place or, better still, imagine being in your favourite place, by the seaside, up in the mountains, in the open air, wherever you please, what's important is that this place makes you happy and relaxed.

Do this until you really feel ready and totally at ease, then open your eyes.

Now you are ready. Enjoy reading.

IDEA

Every day that passes, I read, I keep myself up-to-date and I study, I try to find answers to questions that continue to play on my mind. I wake up every day and try to find out the best ways to live, to love and to love oneself, as well as how many there are. I do not know, but I want to understand. I want to live the little time we are granted intensely, we are just passing through and everything will soon end. Life is the blink of an eye, it flashes past.

I read, I keep myself up-to-date and I study. The Internet and books are my source of information, but it seems nothing and no one is able to give me the answer, so keep looking. One course after another, one book after another. News and details taken from any source of information feed my desire to understand and to mature, to help others and myself, to love and to decide my own fate.

It seems normal and widespread behaviour among people, but it is nothing of the sort. Most of us are in a state of limbo that I call a "hypnotic dream". Created by the media, by trashy programmes and by the feeling that normal, pre-packaged things, made by those who want us all to be the same, leave us with. This is life, it is what they are selling us, it is what living nowadays is.

Not me, I've decided to reject this limbo, this waiting for old age, for death, or for something better that will never happen. We have to build a better future ourselves, day after day. We are the masters of our own fate and we are the only ones who can change it for the better. No one wants to do it for you, no one wants to sacrifice themselves to give you a good life, not me, I want the best, I want the life I deserve.

Everyone I meet has the same primary needs, they all want to live intensely, eat, enjoy themselves and become rich. Many of them have brilliant ideas that fade over the years, many others want to stand out without trying, because it is too difficult to do so, because life is too short and it is best to enjoy it now, immediately, without thinking about tomorrow, and let the rest of the world go to hell!

There is a line in a beautiful song by Vasco Rossi, an Italian singer-songwriter, which always makes me think and says:

"no one gives a damn, as if it were nothing, I would set fire to your house, if it cured my toothache" *.

The famous singer is able to express a very contemporary concept in just a few lines. After many years of meeting people and having to do with them, I have managed to understand an important point. We all have the same identical problem or compression.

We all have a conflict, with ourselves and with our beliefs, which leads us to immediately truncate any idea we may have of freedom and every positive feeling that would give us the drive to live life without limits, without barriers. I decided to write this book to tell the story of eight women, dreamers and down-to-earth types, perhaps imprisoned in their lives, perhaps in search of freedom and an answer.

I thought of them because I love the world of females, I like listening to their stories and I'm always curious about how they think. The world they live in is a modern, contemporary world, consisting of internet and social media. A world made of fast and often superficial contacts. These women are all looking for the sort of happiness that may never appease them, because happiness is not outside their thoughts, but within their souls, the souls of women, often wounded and without certainties.

* "Basta poco" by Vasco Rossi, 2007

We live in this world and the story of these souls is scattered in the various countries I have visited for work reasons. The origins of each protagonist are different, they all live in small to medium-sized towns, all places that are far away from each other, but which share the same "rhythm" of life. Work, family, children, everyday life with its ups and downs.

I asked each of these women to tell their stories first hand, but they all refused my invitation. Perhaps they will do so after this book has been written or perhaps they will never do so. I will let them have the freedom to decide if and when to open their souls to the world.

Hence, it falls to me to tell you of their stories, their lives, in my own words.

Perhaps looking on from afar will paint a faithful picture of what they are like and not how they would like to appear.

ALEASE

It was Easter in the year two thousand and eleven and Alease was already prepared for her splendid day's holiday, a special celebration, the Resurrection celebration. How great it was to get up, it was a pristine day, the sun was warm, though not yet enough to cavort out in the open air. Alease is as radiant as ever, happy, the kids playing in the garden look like blossoming flowers, although no flower has ever made as much noise as they do.

Callie and Ben, the former eight and the latter five years old, are like two rivers in full flow, today they are happy, mum is at home, today there is no work, it is a holiday and it is a spectacular day. Today there is no school, mum is free and all for them.

Alease is forty-two, her children are the fruit of the love, or rather, of the passion she experienced with Leo, who we shall not speak about, since this story is about women.

She has been working in an optician's for many years, she is an expert, she had studied and knows all the tricks of the trade, she lives in Middlesbrough in the UK and knows her job. She has been working in the optical industry for many years and everyone knows that she is good, professional and punctual. She is the best in her field and in her role.

The children play in the garden of the small home where they live with their mum, they are alone, dad isn't there that day, nor would he be there the day after. Dad and mum had quarrelled, again, they had quarrelled for the umpteenth time. Callie had cried and Ben now also cries because he understands, he had grown older and he also cries with the sister who is rearing him. The two siblings care about each other, they love each other. Perhaps dad no longer loved mum, but what do children know about love, passionate, true love.

Indeed, what is true love?

Callie stopped crying, today was a holiday and their grandparents are coming, it's a time to stay together and play.

Alease has Italian blood flowing in her veins. His parents were born in Palermo, Italy, but her life is here, now, in a foreign land where she had found work, where she had studied and where she had found and then lost love. She wants revenge, but now there are the children, having a new love would be difficult, she is tired, she is often alone, even if the grandparents lend a hand. They want to see their little girl happy, they want to see a free woman, but a new love is difficult, everything is complicated and life seems like a leap into the unknown, the future always shrouded in uncertainty.

The day flies past, mass, lunch, games, the grandparents are happy, but they know that their little girl, Alease, is not because she is alone.

She is strong, but not enough to hide what she has inside. Alease is full of anger and frustration, she does not want to admit that maybe she had also made mistakes and should not have fallen for wanting everything immediately, without pondering, without thinking about tomorrow, conscientiously. She was in love and bestowed all her love on her companion who now no longer wants her. She let herself go too fast, without thinking, driven by her impulsiveness.

But by now it was late and life is passing her by, she wants love, true, eternal love.

The Resurrection celebration flew past, it was a beautiful day and it was hot. Celebrations always end too soon and then it's back to the routine. Work, school, children, laundry. But she wants love, everything else is normal life, she doesn't want normality. Alease is looking for something special, something new.

She is at her peak, but the years fly past and she would not be so attractive for ever.

A month has gone since the holidays, Easter is far away and work is as boring as usual, a Thursday like many others, but today is different, today Alease has received a new, unexpected visit, a man, a new customer who needs her skills and experience.

"Good day, what a lovely shop, I would like a new pair of glasses", he says, with the air of an expert. "Hi, I'm Alease, of course, this is a shop that sells glasses", she replies, almost annoyed by the typical "expert" customer and witty remark. However, Alease is in search of love and inside she knows that perhaps her heart is wounded, petrified, switched off. She doesn't want to suffer again.

But that man is different, he seems different, he wants to talk to her, wants to get to know her and seems to ask intelligent, honest, humble questions. While taking a look at the various glasses together, Alease smiles, it has been a long time since she smiled, she jokes, and the witty remark said in first few minutes already seems distant, she is delicate, she wants to live delicately.

When Alease smiles, it's plain to see, she has gorgeous eyes, you can see when she is happy, when she is happy she smiles like when she was little, when she used to play and everyone loved her, when she was little and she smiled it was as if the whole world stopped to stopped to look at her, because she had a contagious, almost magical smile.

"I've made my mind up," he says, "I'll take these, but I'd also like to do something for you", "for me?", says Alease. The man catches her glance and wants that smile to be his, so he asks the smiling Alease if he can immortalise her lips, by taking a picture, a picture he could keep, a picture that would allow him to dream. Alease smiles, blushes and declines the invitation with no trace of anger.

Evening comes, Alease is tired, she goes back home to her children, who are waiting for her and love her.

While at home, alone, Alease begins to think, that man is different, that man was looking for me and the glasses were just an excuse, but perhaps I'm wrong, he's probably like all the others, he'll have me and then he'll dump me. Alease is sad, she wants to be happy, as she had always dreamed of being, but her heart is wounded.

Like all girls of her age, when she was little she would dream of Prince Charming. She slept and dreamt, when she woke up she was happy, smiling, with the sort of smile that only happy girls have, a bright and sunny smile, an easy smile, not false or forced.

When she was little, Alease used to play, just like her children, but she was the little girl, the girl who was playing and always put on a smile to face the day and her youth, like everyone should, happily.

Today is a beautiful day and no one wants to go out, who knows, perhaps even Alease will stay at home, she is looking for love, but fear is stopping her and no one wants to help her reach her goal, no one is with her, but perhaps, just perhaps that man was different. Perhaps.

Saturday is a busy day for Alease, a day in which everything means work for her, and people are in a hurry to do everything with little care and attention, shop assistants are just shop assistants. Alease had studied and is an expert at her job, but in the end, people simply call her a shop assistant, although she is something more, because her expertise has great value, but no one values knowledge, put simply.

It would be a typical day with plenty of customers and people browsing who don't know what to do or where to go, but know exactly why they have gone to see Alease, for a pair of glasses or sunglasses, they have gone to her because they need something, but she is looking for love, nothing else. Not love for her children, that already exists and she gives them plenty, she wants a love that is no longer there, because it has fled from the responsibility of being a father and a man.

What will Alease's life be like tomorrow? It will be what it will be, I hate to think that she will be unable to achieve happiness, but whatever happens, she has given everything, perhaps too much, and had little in return, perhaps nothing.

Alease still lives in Middlesbrough in the UK, has two wonderful children, a job and is single.

She is searching for the love of her life.

MONIQUE

I remember a film, but I don't remember what it was called, I remember that it was modern, of our times, a film with lots of special effects. Of the entire film, the thing I remember particularly is a special effect that occasionally springs to mind. Let me try to explain it in words. The scene begins with a camera shot from far away, almost from infinite space, like the Google Maps home page for example, and slowly begins zooming towards a point on the earth. Then, an increasing level of detail, slowly, more and more. The earth comes closer and the continents become visible, then the states, the mountains, increasingly close, sharper and, slowly, the image continues to come closer, until it's possible to see a figure, a person, a woman with long hair. The shot gets to the face and enters the eyes, Monique's eyes. Her eyes are blue, clear and bright, I sometimes wonder if they are real, they look like the eyes of a waxwork, but they are beautiful, almost hypnotic, and I like to think that they capture the world, so to speak.

She is twenty-four, lives in Nantes in France and her life is different, because she was a beauty queen. Being a beauty queen or an aspiring beauty queen has always prompted a feeling of rejection in me. All these girls presented to the public, almost naked, defenceless. I've always wondered why these young girls are willing to show themselves off at all costs, with the sole aim of achieving success quickly.

How many evenings, how many dreams, and how many auditions, to prove to herself that she was worth something, that she was unique and that everyone had to love her.

Monique has always had a secret dream, but she is still very young. She dreams of becoming someone really important, like a top manager or a famous blogger. She often has conflicting thoughts, because she is never sure what she really wants to do, she is still too young, she will grow older.

After so many disappointments, she now looks happy, she is engaged, has a dog, a job she likes, and lots of dreams to nurture in everyday life. Young and enterprising, always looking for stimuli to do something new. She dreams of living far away, overseas, perhaps in America, where everything seems possible. However, life flies past and perhaps it's best to stay close to home, near where you were born, because in the end you can also fulfil all those dreams at home.

She would like to consume the world, but she risks being devoured by that very same world, she daydreams, but in the end she remains well grounded.

Nowadays, like many women, Monique works in a clothing store, a boutique, full of the most prestigious brands and labels. The same routine every day, new customers every day, but no one knows the true story of Monique. Nobody ever asks her anything, no one really cares about her and her life. We are victims of these modern times, in which everything is a matter of image and few look at you in the face, in the eyes when talking to you.

Her young life has forced her to grow up fast, the auditions, life as a model, taking part in so many beauty pageants, they have made her blossom quickly, without a moment's pause. She was almost forced to skip many phases of her youth. Her desire to grow up fast made her mature, even though she still has a girl's soul.

Her family also made her grow up, the arguments with her mum and dad, her previous love stories, yes, previous, though very young, she went to live away from home when she was only sixteen, a fact mum and dad have never accepted. Perhaps she is right, perhaps her parents are, but that is the story of every family. The new and old generations are unable to communicate, or they don't want to, how many problems would be resolved with words and dialogue, but that's the way of it nowadays, everyone wants to be right. Dialogue between children and parents nowadays is limited to the minimum required for survival. It is the fault of social networks and the web, but above all it is the fault of each individual's will. Try to talk to your parents and your children, arguments lead to nothing.

Is it better to be right or to be happy? Think about that for a moment.

Life is very fast in Nantes, everything is fast and Monique's job certainly doesn't help. Budgets to achieve and an image to maintain are the prerogatives of a high-level shop assistant.

However, perhaps she is happy now that she has found a love and lives with him. I can tell you that she is almost happy, because she often confesses to me, almost in tears: "why doesn't he love me? I'm sure he doesn't love me enough". She complains because she says that her partner does not love her enough, the way he should, the way she dreams he should. Monique is also a victim of her own fears and insecurities, no one understands her and nobody wants to understand her. She would like to run away, go, find her own way, but her current life is as a shop assistant, imprisoned in a job that doesn't excite her, ever.

When she took part in the famous beauty pageant, she had needed and wanted to lose weight, because Beauty Queens mustn't have an ounce of fat, or perhaps she was just not old enough, therefore naturally skinny. After that experience she returned home and also returned to her "normal" shape, which was better and more natural than the impositions dictated by beauty pageants.

Now Monique is thin, too thin, and that's not okay. She'd like to be even thinner and that's even worse. That was the way she wants it and is convinced it means that everyone will love her even more. Though she may be happier now, she is missing love and she never tires of it. Every woman in the world craves being loved, by everyone, forever, but should not be willing to do anything it takes for that to be the case. Monique is too skinny now, I worry about her, she seems to want to disappear from everyone's sight, almost in an attempt to cancel herself out and bring the curtain down, in silence. Before searching for the love of others, love yourself first and foremost.

Monique is a very beautiful girl, she's young, she is still a model, but she doesn't like herself and wants to be something more. However, what she's looking for is already inside her. Her heart, her kindness, affection for her nephew, her beautiful eyes that "hold the world", those are her weapons.

She doesn't think so, she is looking for something more, something that perhaps she will never find.

Broken dreams and the desire to be better have nothing to do with the physical aspect, the image of ourselves that we convey to those who look at us is just passing, because time passes and we all change. Wrinkles, cellulite and white hair are inevitable.

What remains and shall remain of Monique, like all other women, is her congeniality, smile, sweetness and even folly.

Physical appearance is just a passing image that will be replaced by the emotional image we project towards the people around us. Monique projects joy and a joy of life, which are the only things that should be important to her.

Today, Monique lives happily in Nantes, has a job, a boyfriend, a dog, and a beautiful nephew. She hasn't really made up with her parents, they rarely see each other, but she has promised that she will try to forgive them. After all, forgiveness is the first step towards happiness.

She is searching for herself.

MAGDALENA

Talk about fate. I meet this "odd" girl during a summit in Spain, she looks at me and I look at her, our eyes meet, perhaps we study each other. I always look at women, I'm too curious, I like trying to understand what they are like, what they think, why they smile or why they don't smile. They say that curiosity is a female trait, but in my case they are wrong.

She is called Magdalena, lives in Zaragoza in Spain, and is a typical example of a confident woman. Few words, or rather many, in fact now that I think about it too many, she talks and talks and talks, she asks herself questions and gives herself the answers, great fun for someone like me who loves to listen in silence, especially when I'm unable to get a word in edgeways….

After observing each other for a while we manage to have a chat, to get to know each other, to find out if we have anything in common, I like her. She is married, loves cats and animals in general, perhaps that's down to her job, she sells animal food for a large company, so she has to know what she is selling and consequently animals.

Her appearance is important, a woman with a capital "w", but what strikes you the most are her clothing and her accessories, for want of a better word. She wears all kinds of necklaces, earrings, has tattoos on many parts of the body and very eye-catching and flashy outfits. That's how I term it, in the sense of being important, complicated and a little wild.

She is very extroverted, but you can see that she isn't really, she just wants someone to notice her, perhaps to help her find something, perhaps an answer to her questions. She asks lots of questions. Another thing you notice is that Magdalena is very dressed, perhaps too much, it's a hot day, but she is still well covered up. My instinct makes me think of a question knocking around in my head. Why is she wearing so many clothes? Is she trying to hide from something? No, I'm definitely mistaken. It's my usual instinct making me think of something that I can't yet see, who knows.

The expression "like a bolt out of the blue" always makes me smile, because it always occurs to me that I've never seen a bolt of lightning when the sun is shining, so I start wondering who the devil thought up the expression. It certainly hits the mark, but I've always found it funny.

Less fun, or rather, surprising, is when it dawns on you that what a person says to you is more or less exactly what you thought of them before that bolt of lightning struck from the sky.

One day, without warning, Magdalen confesses and knocks down the wall she had built between her and other people, those who watch and judge without knowing her.

At that point, I realise that my instinct is about to take its revenge and claim that it knew all along. "I told you I was right!", it seems to whisper in my ear, "you never trust me, you should listen to me". "Ok, you were right, now shut up and stop going on about it".

As we talk about our routines and work, Magdalena strips herself of her defences and of her layers of clothes, her accessories and all that guarded her from unwanted glances, and confesses.

She wants to say it to the entire world and has decided that now is the time, she vents and asks for understanding.

"I haven't taken my clothes off in front of anyone for more than 10 years, going to the beach is hell and no one must see me in a swimsuit, without my defences. My husband is the only one who is allowed to see me almost naked, in the shade, because I don't like myself".

She continues. "Surgery will ever bring me happiness, my father wanted a boy and my femininity was choked ever since I was a little girl, that is my story, that's what I am".

Then she kneels down and cries, tears of desperation.

You can imagine the shock of hearing such an outburst from a girl I hardly know, but who wants to share something so intimate and important. There's no doubt that the expression "bolt out of the blue" fits like a glove.

The human mind is very complicated, but if aided by instinct it can be accompanied along the path of understanding the things that happen. In this case, shock took over. We poor men are unable to understand and, in this specific case, my brain was unable to understand Magdalena's words.

Such a beautiful girl, a bit bizarre no doubt, but physically almost perfect for her age, has personal issues because of her body? I just can't believe it.

Something doesn't add up, perhaps we've lost the perception or the awareness of what is beautiful and what is less so. However, this girl is beautiful, nice, normal, to all intents and purposes. So, what is the line between beautiful and unacceptable, between ugly and normal?

We are that line, with our unease and our misguided beliefs. Magdalena sees herself like that because she wants to see herself like that, no one in the world except she herself could ever convince her of the opposite. Her father undoubtedly influenced her when she was little and that is unforgivable, of that there is no doubt. Magdalena has to end this nightmare and take back her life.

Each day she gets up and goes to work, a job she loves, but she doesn't love herself, that's the point, and that's what she needs to learn to do. Her father wanted a boy. To hell with her father, this isn't a science fiction film in which you can decide to have a boy or a girl. Magdalena is a woman and has to be loved as such, she must be the first to do so, then the others will follow, if they don't already love her. She alone can choose to be happy right away, her father is an idiot, but she is not her father, I tell her to forgive him and look to the future with her head held high.

Magdalena lives in Zaragoza, has no children, but lots of cats. She is now divorced, but still loves her ex-husband, even though she ruined his life. She wants to undergo breast surgery to look more feminine. She doesn't like herself completely, but she is striving to improve her relationship with the mirror. There's no doubt she'll soon be free of her nightmare.

ANA

It is a beautiful day, the sun warms the skin and even the heart, the shimmering sea and the waves crashing down on the jagged coast seem to embrace the land, in a kind of continuous and imperceptible retreating kiss that transforms the movement of the sea into an eternal and timeless ballet.

Ana lives here, in this city kissed by the sea and open to the world. This coast has fascinated man for many years, once the land of the Romans and the empire of the same name. She is twenty-four years old, a girl whom I affectionately call a "Viking", in the physical sense of the term, tall, very tall, strong, blonde and beautiful. Even her soul is like her, strong and proud. The sea is her home and she has been able to enjoy the mystery that sailors call freedom since she was little. And that is exactly what she is searching for, like so many other women, freedom, to be young, to be herself and to achieve that ultimate goal of happiness.

Ana is strong, she is a professional skipper, at twenty-four years of age she is already capable of sailing a boat in total autonomy and full awareness anywhere she pleases. Her eyes burn with the light of those born in the sea, of those who know and respect it, Ana's look like marine eyes, perhaps more suited to a dolphin than to a woman.

Like every good skipper, Ana has taken part in numerous regattas, lots of crossings and dozens of transfers that have allowed her to develop the confidence and readiness that are essential to providing her guests with a comfortable and exciting holiday at sea.

However, not everything had been so simple. As often happens in the fascinating, yet strange world of sailors, she had also suffered a daft and mindless exclusion by the famous "males", often ignorant and almost always blind to the real abilities of a woman at the helm (the helm, for non-experts, is the steering wheel of a boat).

For many years, Ana offered her services as a professional and skilled skipper to the paying public, only to be rejected for the sole reason of being a woman. "A woman at the helm of a boat? Better to let it drift, it would cause less damage", said the last customer who was asked an opinion.

Ana tells me sadly and almost on the brink of giving up about the number of times she had been called upon for an opportunity of work, only for that hope to vanish, for dozens of pointless and meaningless motives, which would warrant pages and pages of apologies.

However, the world is different from how we see it and sometimes things happen that no one could ever foresee, especially for those who, like Ana, already see themselves relegated to marginal roles, in a world that instead should promote the freedoms of everything and everyone, regardless of who is at the helm.

Summer was here and a couple decide to rent a sailboat on their own. He is almost a skipper, he has a licence and is almost certain he can handle a boat by himself, his partner is single-minded, but clearly inexperienced when it come to sailboats which, even when small, are nothing like city cars, which can be parked at will. The sea is unforgiving and exercising caution is always advisable.

During the trip to the much awaited chartered boat, he begins to prepare his partner for the dream trip they are about to embark upon. How to tie knots, mooring, crucial issues, the wind, what to check for and much, much more, notions and instructions aplenty and the journey by car is soon over.

They had already been in a sailboat, but somebody else had skippered it, now was the time to do the business, all alone, in the open sea.

Upon reaching the rental location, they see the boat and the tension begins to climb, to the extent that he understands that perhaps he is not yet ready, then a flash of genius strikes him. "Why don't we hire a skipper for a few days? Perhaps that would be better, so we'll have the time to understand if we're really good enough to sail". No sooner said than done. The rental company immediately starts looking for a skipper and shortly afterwards informs the two holidaymakers that they are lucky because in the high season there is normally no one available at the last minute, but there is a small problem or two.

The first problem is that the skipper is not available immediately for departure, but only the following morning, and the second is that the skipper is a woman...

The rental operator is almost about to call the female skipper and tell her that there is no need, that there would be a negative outcome this time, too. A colleague of the operator begins to explain what the skipper is like, that she is a great person, takes part in lots of regattas, is sweet, kind and discreet, then the man stops her.

"Excuse me," says the customer, "what's the problem? I've already decided she's fine, no problem, you can guarantee for her and, regardless of whether she is male or female, all I'm interested in is whether she can sail a boat, no more no less, there's no need for any other explanation". The operator apologises and enthusiastically calls the skipper, who would take the couple on a great adventure at sea the very next day.

The trip was fantastic, the morning after Ana's arrival, the couple embarked and spent seven, unforgettable days (the initial agreement with the skipper had only been for three days), full of fun and new discoveries.

The most beautiful feeling for the couple was to have given a woman of that ability, despite her young age, the opportunity to express her knowledge and seamanship, without prejudice and without obstacles, finally free.

Nowadays, Ana lives in Zara or Zadar in Croatia, where she was born. She is still a Viking, even stronger, with even more awareness.

Since the couple gave the rental company their feedback on her seamanship skills, Ana has worked as a skipper, like never before.

She is happy, she no longer has a boyfriend. She's trying to grow up in the world she loves, the sea.

THE WORLD

The world has made great strides in recent decades and women have become stronger, more independent, but at the same time more vulnerable. Their exposure and the fact that they tend to be more aggressive, to take back what was wrongly wrested from them in the past, has turned them into different people, undoubtedly to be admired, but in another way surreptitiously fearsome. Their reawakening and their desire achieve make the men of today appear weaker and like children, overwhelmed by a feminine force emerging from the past.

What is a woman, what is she looking for, what does she want to be, what are her goals? Such questions surface at any time during my day in which I see, speak to or discuss things with women of all kinds, young and old, mothers, fiancées, friends and workers, often ironic and always mysterious.

Women are always an exciting discovery, sometimes you hate

them so much that you wish they didn't exist, then in a flash they make you forgive them and are capable of touching the chords that render them indispensable. Careful mothers, tireless workers who are invariably becoming the drivers of their families and of life itself.

I am always struck by their strength and determination, sometimes it shocks me, because I've never been like that in my life and nor have many others, I would imagine.

There is a well-known advertisement for a chocolate snack that I really like, which shows a typical day of a woman with a husband and children, a housewife who also holds down a job. It seems exaggerated, but in truth it mirrors the life of an active mother, of which there are many. Breakfast, then the children, school, lunch, work, pilates and colleagues to compete with. Then dinner in the evening... and finally the husband, who is often tired because he has worked all day.

At the end of her day, she is offered an energising snack and the day turns into a breeze. So the only thing capable of recharging her is the chocolate bar? Trivial? Perhaps not. Perhaps it only takes little to help a woman, perhaps all that's needed is some sweetness and a little bit more care and attention. After all, what does it take to give someone a little bit of sweetness, you just need to want to do so.

A woman overcomes these adversities as if they were nothing

and manages to transform herself into Wonder Woman, even at the most difficult times, in the blink of an eye. What is the secret of these special beings? Where do they find the strength to overcome almost anything?

From which ancestral source of energy are they able to gather the strength to overcome any adversity?

PIERCARLA

Speaking of strong women, let me tell you about Piercarla, a very strong, unique and great woman.

A mother of two children, a selfless wife, hard worker and faithful participant in the religious life of her parish. She was born in the countryside, to a family of farmers, a traditional family of the past. I'm always reminded of the film, "The Tree of Wooden Clogs", when thinking of this beautiful family. They all live in a big house, there is a vegetable garden, fields that need to be worked, hens, a cow, almost a complete farm.

Since she was a child she has always been used to working, to helping out at home, to looking after her younger siblings and, first her studies, then her work, have always kept her busy. The family, which grew up on a diet of bread and sacrifices, has always stayed together, even in the face of difficulties, the seasons with poor harvests and all the problems that only those who work the land can comprehend.

Piercarla grows up and decides to find a job that is different to the one of her family of origin, an office job, which makes her grow and mature, a job that she likes and that fascinates her, as a woman and as a hard worker.

Then she finds love, marriage, children and life goes on. Unfortunately, life sometimes plays tricks, especially on those who do not deserve them, and Piercarla gets sick, at fifty-two years of age, in the space of a few months, Piercarla passes away, consumed by the tumour that struck her down, at her peak on this earth.

Piercarla was my cousin, but I hadn't seen her for years due to the distance and laziness. Life has a habit of making people drift apart and then only draws us back together again in sad times.

Just before Easter 2017, I went to the hospital to visit her, to say hello, to cheer her up and to provide her with a few minutes of smiles and memories. She was smiling and wanted to go home, she was tired, but strong, like only a woman can be in those moments, incredibly strong. When I went to visit her, she almost didn't recognise me, we hadn't seen each other for years and it was undoubtedly a pity that we had not seen more of each other, every so often, but now it's too late.

"Is that you?", she asks. In reply, I put on my best smile and answer, "it's me, older, but it's still me". She smiles and, incredulous, she kisses me and we hug. I'm supposed to be here to cheer her up, yet I almost feel bad as she says lots of nice things about me, that I'm as attractive as ever, that I'm very young and look good with long hair, a bit of a scoundrel, like our uncle, she says. I'm almost embarrassed and her compliments are so sincere that they cheer me up and give me hope that she will get better, still confident, still positive, as I always am, it doesn't cost me anything, and she needs it, it shows.

She's lying on the bed, she's very tired and her face is dull, but she tries to smile. Piercarla perhaps doesn't know her true state of health, but I don't care, I'm certainly not going to ruin her day, she's smiling, she's happy, let's allow her to smile, to be happy, to be relaxed, that all I can do, nothing more.

I brought her presents, which I use as an excuse to change the subject and not talk about her condition. "I've brought you two presents", I say, "some books".

She looks at me almost astonished, we haven't seen each other for years and she tries to understand what the hell I'm saying. "Yes, I've brought you two beautiful books to read", I repeat. She confesses that she can no longer read, because she's too tired, I worry and in that instant understand the seriousness of the situation, which for some is very clear, but not for me, because I don't know the truth, it seems like a lie, almost a useless, mysterious alarm. My trademark positivity often doesn't allow me to see the real problems, or perhaps doesn't let me to see those that are impossible to solve. "Come off it", I tell her, "you can read a page a day, slowly, even if you're tired. Come on, pull yourself up, they're beautiful, it will make you happy". I feel powerless, but I don't want her to sense it and continue my presentation.

"The first book is the story of a girl, a strong woman like you, who managed to do something extraordinary, she single-handedly circumnavigated the world in a sailboat. A woman who managed a great endeavour, just as you will by getting better and going home to your family, tired but victorious, stronger than before".

Then I continue. "The other book I want to give you is a beautiful and engaging story about a couple of friends, Carlo and Elisabetta, who sailed the seven seas and give a spectacular description of their journey. It's a beautiful story, reading it will take you to places you've never seen before and it will definitely make you feel better".

As I describe the books I brought her, I smile and get excited, because I love the sea and I would like to stay with her and read them, but she can't read because she's unable to, she's very tired. She promises to take the time to read them, tells me that if I'm not in a hurry she will give them back to me when she goes home, then she smiles and I smile, we've understand each other, without the need for further words.

 Before saying goodbye after three hours of chat, memories and laughter, I serve her dinner, some soft cheese, two boiled carrots and some water.

Before I leave, I ask her if I can open the curtains a little, it's a wonderful day outside, the sun is shining, the room is hot and stuffy, I open the window, open the curtains and the light streams in, she smiles and thanks me, she seems reborn. What a strong woman, a rock, like only a woman knows how to be.

I promise her I'll be back to visit, after Easter.

I make up an excuse, I tell her that I'm often in the area for work over the next few days, so it will be easy to come and visit her, so as not to alarm her, to make her understand that we'll see each other often, to make her understand that there is time.

15 days after my visit, Piercarla passed away, in silence, on tiptoes, leaving a husband, two children and many friends.

I just hope I made her smile and gave her a few hours of relief.

There were hundreds of people at her funeral, relatives and many friends. The silence and composure reflected what Piercarla had been, a strong woman.

Piercarla lived in Padua, Italy.

Goodbye cousin, you'll give me those books back when we meet, take all the time you need to read them.

CHARLOTTE

There are days when you don't want to do anything and others when you want to do everything, you dream that everything happens on that day and that it will be the most beautiful of your life, nothing and nobody can stop you. I call them "recharging" days.

Days like these can cancel out the last three months, perhaps studded with bad luck and even worse moods. "Recharging" days can wipe away the dust deposited on our souls by work, stress, angry friends, traffic, news programmes (avoid watching them) and by all those small, but persistent niggles that seem to be created by some evil little devil who wants to keep us constantly under pressure, for whatever strange reason.

The truth lies elsewhere, because while it's true that the things that happen around us tend to influence our existence, often it is the way in which we confront interferences that makes us decide whether we are unassailable or vulnerable. The choice is ours alone.

Charlotte likes recharging days, she is often vulnerable and my beautiful words have no influence on her, she decided to be vulnerable, but perhaps it's the type of wound that has made her so weak. She lives with Leo, they met in Denville, New Jersey, when she was still at high school. It all started with a few glimpses on the subway, glances, and then that day when he asked her to go to the café close to home for a chat and to talk about this and that. That's what Leo always used to say, let's talk about this and that over a coffee.

As the days went by, Charlotte became fond of him and, over time, she fatally fell in love. When Charlotte talks to her friends about her love, it's like she's describing a novel.

Their first meeting at the café, the first kiss, the evenings at the pizzeria, at Lake Wildwood, always together and always in love. He was as romantic, like Romeo in the famous Italian story of Romeo and Juliet. Their love appeared true, transparent and engaging to everyone. A phone call, a kiss, a thought, every day.

Charlotte's friends know her well, she is considered the romantic of the group. Her friends always enjoy hearing her stories and they are close to Charlotte and the love and passion that she feels for Leo.

Is love contagious?

What's the best day in a woman's life? Some says it's her wedding day, but I've never understood why.

For Charlotte that day has arrived today, she is getting married to Leo. After four years of engagement and three months of living together, she has decided to marry her Prince Charming, perhaps it's a little early, she's young, but as modern girls say, who cares, she's decided to get married and that's what she's going to do.

Charlotte's mother, a widow, would like to make her daughter understand that love needs to be cultivated over time and that you can only truly know someone after living together for long enough.

Charlotte's mother, Victoria, says, "I loved your father for many years until his death, but I never really knew him deep down, I discovered things I thought I knew every day. Trust me, my daughter, take the necessary time and you will understand when the time is really right".

It was like talking to a brick wall, Charlotte was stubborn as her father and would not have listened to her mother's wise words. "You know mum," says Charlotte, "Leo and I have known each other for many years, he loves me, cares for me, gives me flowers and always takes me to the nicest and most romantic places. And then there's the ring, that ring made me take the right decision, were getting married, yes, we're getting married on the tenth of September, and our love will last forever".

The day came and everything went perfectly, the marriage she had always dreamed of, beautiful, joyous, friends and relatives, just a few people, but all dear and close to Charlotte. She was beautiful, a princess, a flower. The dream had come true and Charlotte had finally reached the height of her love, she was happy and finally satisfied.

On the twenty-third of November of the same year, early in the morning, someone knocks on the door of the apartment where Charlotte and Leo lived.

He goes to open the door and finds their next door, Mrs Lydia, a pleasant and often curious old lady who knows everyone in the building. In Denville, everyone knows everyone else in the same building, unlike the big cities in which people hardly even say hello and the neighbours could just as well be serial killers, for all anyone else knows.

Mrs Lydia always felt it was important, so she brought every newcomer her trademark apple pie, which was tasty, but often too sweet, as a welcome gift. Mrs Lydia uses loads of sugar, she says she wants to sweeten the lives of her guests, she thinks of the building as a ship and the other tenants are her passengers.

Strangely annoyed, Leo asks the lady why he had knocked on his door, so early in the morning and on a Saturday, to boot. His unexpected and inappropriately harsh question was: "What the hell do you want Lydia? It's early in the morning and I'm tired, go back to bed!".

Lydia had known the couple for a few months, but she had never heard Leo talk that way. While it's true that they had rarely spoken to each other, he seemed like a good boy, calm and polite, perhaps just a little on the quiet side. Mrs Lydia was part of a bygone generation, in which personal relationships were nurtured day after day and people knew each other very well.

"I passed by because I was worried," says the elderly lady. "Last night I heard shouting from your apartment and not wanting to disturb anyone, I thought that perhaps someone was sick, then the shouting stopped and I waited until morning to see if everything was ok". While Lydia is talking, like a cat fleeing from a mouse, Charlotte passes through the corridor leading to the bathroom and covers her face, crying. Then, she quickly go enters the bathroom and closes the door, turning the key as many times as it would go, as if to seal the door.

"Go away," Leo says, "everything's ok, go back to sleep, it's early morning, mind your own business!".

When you think you know a person because you have talked to them for a few minutes on the stairs of the landing, but you don't have time to get to know them properly, at some point in the future you will realise that you don't really know them at all and the image you had created disappears in a matter of seconds.

Many times we catch ourselves saying I know him or I know her. However, knowing someone is a prerogative of a deeper understanding, of sharing experiences, above all negative experiences, which bring out the true character in people, what they are, not what they appear to be. The speed of the modern world often leads to us making this mistake, we think we know someone just because they are our "friend" on Facebook, while the truth is that there are very few people who we really know. And even with the few that we think we know really well, we still don't have the certainty of knowing what they truly think. It takes a lifetime to really understand someone and even that's not enough. The question "are we friends on Facebook?" is truly absurd. What on earth does it mean, that we're not friends outside the digital world? Perhaps yes, perhaps that's the reality, the word 'friends' almost seems like a saying.

In that precise moment, as she left the landing of the young couple, Mrs Lydia realised that this was the case. "I don't know Leo", she repeated, returning to her home. "I don't know him, but perhaps this morning I've understood a little more about him, I think he is a nasty man, he is no longer the pleasant and sweet Leo I had imagined, how stupid I am". Lydia is not stupid, Lydia is an elderly lady who only wants what's best for everyone and still believes in love.

After a few hours, Charlotte goes to work, she takes the subway and, during the trip, she gets lost in thought. The day is the same as many others, with colleagues and tasks to carry out, today is a strange day, everything seems in slow motion, it seems like a day of transition and change.

The hours at work pass quickly, it's time to go back and, in the evening, Charlotte is about to go home, but something stops her. She doesn't want to go back, she's daunted, confused and doesn't want to go back to Leo.

Charlotte is scared.

When love is broken and dreams turn into nightmares, the only thing you can do is change course, cut off the dead branches. Like a good sailor in the middle of the sea, you need to avoid going against a storm, at the first clear signs of bad weather, change course, to avoid going back and to avoid disaster.

Women often fail to change course, they "prefer" to go towards the storm, at the risk of drowning, because they can't accept defeat, they believe in love and their choice cannot be questioned.

Charlotte begins to ask herself a thousand questions and her mind starts to harbour doubts. "What will my friends say, what will my relatives think, how will my mother react? How will it reflect on me, what if it's my fault? And she continues, "What have I done,

I must have done something to deserve this, I must have said something, what will everyone say?".

I have an answer to all these questions and it is: who gives a damn!

The thought of so many women in the world letting themselves be mistreated by their man, for reasons that I do not understand and cannot even begin to conceive, drives me mad. These women seem imprisoned in a cage without escape, stunned, helpless. To avoid any doubt, I'm talking about mistreatment and domestic violence. There's a need for justice and exemplary punishments, that's the only way to curb the problem.

Who cares what friends say, who cares what relatives say, who cares what anyone says, who cares. It's your life, don't let what others might say influence you, who cares!

Charlotte is twenty-seven years old, nowadays she lives in Morristown, not far from Denville, with her mother. She left Leo that very night that she decided not to return home from work. He had begun to mistreat her and had even beaten her sometimes, as early as the first day after their marriage, out of jealousy, madness, nobody knows, we don't care. Leo is a wretched person and showed himself for what he really is, an idiot.

Charlotte had the courage to leave without looking back. Charlotte is a strong girl who has understood that it is her life and nobody can mistreat her, nobody.

Her friends respect and protect her, her motto has become: "Who cares". Good for you, Charlotte!

I hope that many women, upon reading this book, will take courage and make the right decision for their own happiness.

HOW MANY TIMES

There are plenty of times I would like to help someone I don't know reach their goals, but as often happens, help is seen as personal interest. Very few people know how to ask for help and even fewer accept it, they see help as an investment by those who give it, a silent and rational exchange, if I help you, you will have to repay me in some way.

That is undoubtedly the most difficult obstacle to overcome for those in need of support and is actually defensible.

Every time someone takes on the responsibilities and privileges of approaching a person in need, they should, so to speak, confess their inclination towards charity and to the fact that they don't want anything in return, a sincere thanks is more than enough.

Nowadays, the world revolves around commerce and the fact that everything has to be part of an exchange. It's as if feelings are for sale, they seem to have adopted this modern lifestyle, which is not so modern after all. The hard work of hundreds of years, done by our predecessors to teach us to share, enjoy and love our neighbour, is being lost and the values that remain are those of "do ut des" and nothing more. It's sad and empty, but I am still a believer, the world will understand that not everything is based on trade and exchange, I'm still a believer.

If the world today finds itself in this situation, filled with tensions and ill-feeling, this is one of the reasons.

Personally, I have unfortunately come to realise, I have often offered people help, clearly without asking for anything in return. In addition to physical and moral help, often I have also given help in the form of money. The result has been very disappointing. In addition to perhaps losing a "friend", I have been criticised for not having helped enough or, at least, to a lesser extent than expected.

What will happen in future if we continue with this approach? Simply and sadly, the hearts of people will waste away.

If you don't think my help is sufficient, no matter how little it may be, then why should I give any at all? We should be grateful for even the seemingly most insignificant gestures, we should applaud these angels, we should praise their deeds, however small, however fleeting, but nevertheless useful to improve our lives.

NICOLE

Without a shadow of doubt, when the day begins on the wrong foot, due to inertia or other reasons, the day continues in the same vein and with the same shower of bad luck. So what if it's a bad day, it will pass and another will take its place, no doubt compensating the one that has just been. "Life was like a box of chocolates, you never know what you're gonna get" *.

Nicole lives like that, as if every morning she opens a box of chocolates, a new one every day, full of mystery, that's what she's like, a bit fatalist. Ah, how nice it would be to be able to right certain days, yet they tend to bow to the will of destiny and of how we began them. The day always follows the direction that we have impressed upon it, since the morning, as soon as we awake.

*from the film Forrest Gump, 1994

For Nicole, today is the last day of work before leaving for her long-awaited holiday.

The departure has already been decided, everything is ready, tomorrow morning, whatever happens, she will get on that plane, which will take her to Istanbul, Turkey. She has dreamed of a holiday in that country for years and, despite friends and colleagues advising her to change destination, like every morning she takes the day as it comes and resolutely wants to reach her holiday destination. A new experience in a country that is new to her and from which she expects a lot.

Nicole lives in Kumla, Sweden, she recently graduated in communication science and has always dreamt of travelling the world. She works at a small school where they do private lessons for students who need help and support and her passion is helping youngsters, free of charge, although the owner of the school gives her something, because Nicole is good and clearly she clearly appreciates her. It is thanks to this pay that her dream of travelling is about to become a reality. Nicole wants to go alone, she is very young, but she is not scared, she sees every day as a new discovery, which she wants to see on her own, without external influences, without any bother, as young people say today.

The evening before departure, the sun had strangely dimmed earlier than expected, in the sense that the clouds had almost obscured it, before the normal time for sunset.

How strange, summer is almost here, yet that sunset resembled winter more than it did summer. Nicole had noticed, she is fatalistic, but she likes to look at the sky, nature and the sun, these things are not lost on her.

Few people are able to perceive and appreciate what nature can tell us during every moment of the day. People are often so distracted by the background noise that they do not realise what's staring them in the face, a bright sun, the wind, nature changing daily. Everything seems the same and repetitive for those who do not know or do not want to look at the world with nature's eyes. Take a moment tonight, watch the sunset, look at the moon, dream.

Her suitcase is ready, just a few things, "I'm only staying a few days, anyway ", thinks Nicole. "It's best to travel light, the train ride to the airport, then the flight and all the rest. Yes, it's best to travel light. The flight is quite quick, only a couple of hours, a couple of hours fly past, I won't even notice".

 "A short nap and we'll be in Istanbul. How thrilling, I might not even be able to close my eyes during the flight".

Nicole's father, Matías, has always pushed her to have new experiences, has always urged her to travel, to look for what she considers right, to achieve her purpose in life. As a child, Matías often took her on trips during the weekends, to the lake to fish or to the sea.

Nicole loves the sea, it makes her feel free and sad at the same time, it reminds her of when she was little, without worries, without a care in the world and back when dad was her best friend and accomplice.

Nicole thinks life is great, she is always happy, everything revolves around her and her youth was giving her plenty. Like every girl of her age, confusion often stirred her nights and even her days, since she was fatalistic, she could never establish a real goal that she wanted to achieve, at school, at work, in her travels, something was always missing, love was missing.

Her first crush was when she was in middle school, she was little and did not understand that it was just a passing crush, because the crush was on her PE teacher, Paul. The typical young, good-looking and likeable teacher.

The hour of Physical Education is also the best lesson is, not for everyone, though, and girls often try to avoid it for a thousand reasons, especially physical ones, since they are at a particular age, when their bodies are transforming and they become terribly shy.

Nonetheless, Nicole took part in almost every lesson, because she liked the hour of PE, she had no issues with her body, she felt at ease with her body and that crush undoubtedly helped her young spirit to overcome the obstacle of shyness.

The teacher was particularly "athletic" that day and Nicole's eyes sparkled at the mere thought of being near her favourite teacher. During a series of exercises, the teacher stops the class and asks everyone to hurry up and end the day's programme, because, unfortunately, he had to finish the day's lesson ten minutes early. "You know, my new partner is coming to pick me up here at school today and I don't want to make her wait," explains Paul.

Nicole almost jealously gives the teacher an angry look, but he doesn't even notice, after all, he's completely unaware of Nicole's feelings, and nor could it be otherwise, given the age difference. Just before the end of the lesson, someone knocks on the door of the gym, a young student peers in and calls the teacher. "There's a lady waiting at the entrance, I didn't know what to do so I came to call you".

The teacher hurries up and tells the students that the lesson is over. "Put away the equipment and the balls, then go and get changed, see you at the next lesson".

Everyone hurries to clear up, the teacher heads out, but Nicole, who is jealous and curious, wants to see who stole her boyfriend, according to her. Her thoughts gallop quickly.

She follows him without being seen, while the teacher goes to the school entrance, where his new partner is waiting for him. Paul seems worried, and this meeting makes him very nervous, maybe it's his first real date, maybe he's shy.

Nicole is like a detective and manages to follow the teacher without being noticed, she sees him leave, but does not see the girl who is already outside and kisses him, a girl with dark, long hair. She looks like a beautiful woman, no longer very young, but she looks pretty, she must be around forty-five, thinks Nicole, hoping that her rival is a dribbling, old woman with a limp.

Nicole returns to the changing rooms, disappointed and a bit defeated by her rival in love. "Who knows what that woman's face is like, I couldn't see it", she thinks, "I bet she's ugly", even though there was nothing to say that was the case. Nicole is jealous, she would like to eliminate her rival, with a click of the fingers.

Going home from school that morning, Nicole kept thinking about what she had seen and, in her mind, she began to make up stories and assumptions about her rival, and how she could make the teacher understand that she loved him, that she was the love of his life, not that lady, who was too old for him, too grown up. The imagination of teenagers is an astonishing weapon, they are able to create incredible stories by daydreaming, then their dreams blow over as time passes and real life begins. It's a pity, it would be nice to dream all the time.

"Hello mummy! I'm home!". When she came home, Nicole always liked to say hello to her mum first thing, even if her mum was not at home, she always likes to say hello to her mum in a strong and happy voice, because mum must always be happy, according to Nicole every mum in the world should always be greeted with a smile.

Nicole's mother is a beautiful lady, always kind and helpful towards the whole family, especially her favourite Nicole, Fred, Nicole's older brother, and Matías, her husband and the children's father.

Every time Nicole talks about her daddy, she always recollects the trips to the lake, or the swims in the sea, and all the hours spent travelling and having fun with him, the best dad in the world. Nicole and Matías have always been accomplices and the memories remain etched in the girl's mind, like indelible writings.

After lunch that day Nicole's mum, having finished the housework, wants to talk to her about some news regarding the family. Fred is already old enough, so she will explain everything to the older of the two children later on, the priority now is Nicole, she is sensitive and her mum knows it all too well.

"Nicole", her mum begins, "there are moments in life when you have to make choices, even if they are painful, because they are necessary and putting them off would be much worse than facing them straight away".

Nicole listens and smiles, she thinks her mum just wants to give her the usual mother's advice, perhaps to put more effort in at school or to be careful with the boys, the usual things, and that she is just going through the usual sugar-coated premise to prepare her for the bitter pill of her reproach.

"Nicole", her mum continues, "perhaps you will hate me now, but when you grow up you will excuse me, youngsters don't understand these things, but you're intelligent and you will undoubtedly understand".

"Mum!", Nicole calls her mother loudly, "What on earth is going on? Has the cat died by chance?" Grinning, Nicole thinks, "we don't have a cat".

"Nicole", urges her mum, "you need to know that your dad and I have been having a few problems for a while, love changes over the years and things change, Nicole, your father and I don't love each other like we used to and we've decided to split up".

When there is a total solar eclipse, at a certain point for a few seconds the world around us seems as if it were blocked, obscured, petrified. A total eclipse of sun was forming inside Nicole's head. Her head had emptied and her expression was that of a fawn that had been abandoned by its mother in the forest, in the freezing cold.

I think the most painful thing for a young girl is to witness her parents splitting up. I don't mean that at a more mature age the situation is less traumatic or superficial, but the youthful years in which a girl grows up and becomes a woman are part of a very vulnerable period from the emotional point of view. Separations should be avoided, if possible. The separation of two parents also results in separation from friends and moving away from all that is happiness and security.

In recent years I have been interested in studying the people's souls, their feelings and reactions to external stimuli. Among the various things I have learnt, and that I wish to mention here, is the fact that in life there are only two truly irreplaceable persons. A father and a mother, each one of us will only have one mum and one dad in our lives, which makes them precious and unique.

Nicole is stunned by the news, her mum and her dad want to split up and become, so to speak, single, like they used to be, as if nothing had happened, as if their family and children had never existed, just like that, with a click of the fingers.

Nicole's mum understands that the news has not been received by the girl as she had expected, so she tries to justify herself. "You know, sweetheart, things change, love changes, with the passing of time people are capable of neutralising years of happiness and good times, it happens, that's life".

Nicole recovers and, like a scared little animal that is still able to react, asks her mum: "do you have a new boyfriend?". Her mum blushes, steps back and uses an excuse to disappear. "I'm going to do the laundry", she says, "it's late, go to bed, we'll talk about it tomorrow, when things have settled a bit".

Nicole immediately understands that her mother is lying to her. "There's another man in mum's life, I don't want that, I want my happy family, like it was before, like it's always been".

"I'm not having this", she continues to repeat to herself, realising that she can't do anything about it, what will happen is what was meant to happen.

The next day Nicole, who had been unable to sleep that night, gets up early in the morning and wants to know if what she had heard from her mother last night had been real. "Perhaps I dreamt it", she thought, "perhaps it was all a nightmare". The only way for her to understand if her parents' relationship was really over was to check if they were still sleeping in the same bed. So, stealthily, she wanted to check her parents' room to see if both were in there, which would have been a positive note for her, confirmation that she had misunderstood and that perhaps the night before had been just a bad nightmare with her eyes open.

In order to peek into her parents' room, Nicole first had to leave her own room, passing in front of her brother's room, in the corridor. The door to Fred's bedroom is always left open: from an early age, due to a trauma, he had always wanted to sleep with the door practically wide open. Unlike many teenagers who want absolute privacy and shut themselves in their rooms, he preferred the "safety" of an open door.

Nicole approaches her big brother's room, he's sleeping, she passes almost without breathing, she doesn't want to be caught and then teased by her favourite brother. Then she walks silently and arrives almost in front of her parents' room. "How can I do this?", she thinks, "they're inside, they're sleeping, so if I open the door they'll hear me and my plan will be ruined". What are you doing in our room? Are you ill? "How embarrassing, no, I have to change strategy, this isn't going to work".

While Nicole thinks of her new strategy and backs away from her parents' door, she hears a noise from the ground floor, gets agitated and is worried. "Crikey, there are thieves downstairs, what should I do?". In the fear of the moment, she brings both hands to her mouth, as if to stifle a cry of terror that she was about to let out.

The family house is very large, on the ground floor there is a beautiful room to the left of the entrance, preceded by a waiting room. On the right, facing dad's study, is a large kitchen with a very broad and bright window overlooking the garden, a bathroom nearby and a door to go out into the garden. The bedrooms are on the first floor, the large one belongs to mum and dad and two smaller ones are for her and Fred. Nicole hears more noises from the kitchen and thinks, "these thieves are stealing our apples from the fridge, what kind of thieves are they? Hungry thieves, who knows?". Then, still frightened and somewhere in between shouting and fainting, she hears an unmistakable sneeze, "it's dad's sneeze, it's him, it's unmistakable!".

Exhaling forcefully, as if to drive the fear from her stomach, she silently takes the stairs to the ground floor, heading for the kitchen.

"Dad? What are you doing up at this time and, more to the point, eating chocolate and crackers?". Nicole's father, half asleep, but already smiling, answers, "Haven't you heard the news Nicole, sweetheart, I live in the living room now and I got up to have a snack, I was hungry, last night before you came home your mum told me that she had only made dinner for you and Fred. So I went to bed without any dinner. Then, when your mother came to bed, she kindly asked me to go and sleep in the living room, since our relationship was over, so here I am, aching from sleeping badly on the couch and starving from having missed dinner, which is just great".

The last glimmer of hope Nicole had of seeing her parents fall back in love like before vanished. A tear almost crept out of her eye, but she, so strong and so proud, did not want to aggravate an already sad situation. "My life is over", she thought, "love doesn't exist, either".

As her father continued to eat his breakfast-dinner, Nicole began to think in a concentrated and mature manner about how this disaster could have happened. Who betrayed who? Not mum, she's too nice, my insinuation last night was undoubtedly wrong, I asked her if she had a new boyfriend, I'm a fool. Dad is nice, too, though. Yes, but he's a man and everyone knows men are pigs, my friend Diana always say so and she already knows about men and has already had experiences of "reconnaissance". She says that all men are the same, pigs, who only think about enjoying themselves with girls, then move on to others.

"That's not the case with my father, he's different, I've known him since I was born", Nicole thinks, smiling, in a flash of clarity and almost joy.

"What's happened dad, why have you split up? Haven't you thought about us, is there anything I can do?". The most powerful question had not yet surfaced, that morning, which had begun strangely, too early. "Dad, tell me, do you have another woman?".

The few seconds that passed between the question and the answer seemed to take forever. Nicole entire young life flashed before her eyes in those seconds, smiles, family, happiness, few or almost non-existent quarrels between her parents, had crowned her life as a daughter and a girl until now. "Tell me dad. I want to know, if you've decided to live with another woman that's fine, but mum loves you, we love you, why, why, don't do it, please".

The tears that had previously just brushed Nicole's moist eyes, suddenly began to stream down her face, like a waterfall. As well as the tears, sobs also began to interrupt the unreal silence that hovered in the kitchen of their home that morning.

"You're crying, sweetheart", says Nicola's father, "you never cry. A study has found that women live longer because they cry more often than us men, it makes the heart feel good, so the studies say, so cry, let it all out, you'll feel better afterwards".

After soaking a few handkerchiefs with tears, Nicole sits next to her father and softly repeats the question. "Tell me why you're leaving mum, what has she done to you, weren't you happy? Is it my fault? Have I done something wrong?".

Nicole appears to want to take all the blame, perhaps she wants to prove to herself that everything can be sorted out in some way, that love still exists.

Her father looks at her half amazed and half amused, then confesses.

Nicole's father has always been one of those people you could give your house keys to, a reliable man, always smiling and ready to help anyone. Sometimes it looks like he was born to help others. He always finds a solution to everything and his knowledge of the world makes him an interesting and single-minded person.

Every time someone in the family had a problem or needed help, they knew they could count on him. The son of a warehouseman, he had studied as an accountant, first at high school and then at the Economics faculty at university, and then landed a much sought after job as finance manager at a large commercial company.

His life had always been characterised by a mixture of joy and melancholy, a simple man, very grounded, in love with life, friends and happy times. Some might call him an inert man, but what is the true definition of a man like him? Would it be better to live with a man who turns people's lives into nightmares? Many women are attracted to good-looking men who are bastards and it is undoubtedly the fault of their subconscious, which tries to feed off emotions, whether positive or negative.

What emotional food do we want to feed our subconscious?

"Sweetheart", continues Matías, "I love you dearly and I would do anything to make you happy, I love your brother, too, but you are my little girl and I would never wish to disappoint you. I love you more than I love myself and living away from you already seems like a nightmare that I don't even want to think about. You're still little and the things I'm about to tell you will hurt you, but they are necessary to make you understand who your mother really is".

Last February, your mother and I were in the clothes shop on the corner near the fast food restaurant, you know, where we go and eat together from time to time. We were looking for something clothes for me, your mum was a little nervous, more than normal, but at first I thought nothing of it. Women are often nervous, it's part of their nature. At one point, I see her hectically messaging on the phone. You know that your mum doesn't use the phone much, but that day she seemed absorbed, she didn't even look at me while I was trying on the shirts and jackets, she seemed absent. At one point, she looked annoyed and told me she was hot, which is odd in February, it seemed absurd, and she told me: "I'm going to the fast food restaurant to get a cool drink, you try on some clothes, then we'll take a look at them together". It seemed incredible to me, your mum seemed like a different person.

I didn't think of it at the time, but your mother was clearly talking to someone on the phone, and it was obvious, in hindsight, that it was a man.

The minutes passed and your mother didn't return, I became anxious and suspicious, I was afraid that may have been ill, it all seemed very strange, I was worried, I called her on the phone, but she didn't answer.

Shortly after I left everything in the shop and told the shop assistant that I would be back soon. I got dressed and headed towards the fast food restaurant. I approached the entrance, but just before entering I saw your mum through the window of the restaurant, from behind, talking to a person, so I calmed down, she was fine, I was about to go in when, when….

"Dad, what's wrong with you, why are you crying?", asks Nicole, seeing her father turn pale and starting to cry, "what did you see, dad, tell me, please, what did you see".

Her father takes a breath and braces himself, wiping the tears from his face.

"Sweetheart, I saw your mother with a man, they were kissing".

In that same instant, the first light of dawn touched the kitchen table and the fine dust that is always present in the air became "noticeable", so to speak, thanks to the rays of the sun. Time had stopped. It seemed like the earth had stopped turning and everything became muffled. Nicole felt deaf, almost asleep, incredulous, disappointed, dazed.

In a matter of seconds, all her certainties, her dreams and her hopes had disappeared. Something that had never existed, a new and unexpected feeling, as if someone had confessed a secret to her that no one in the world knew. In those few seconds, Nicole had become aware and, so to speak, grown older.

By now the two of them had been talking for almost an hour and the first sounds of the day began to be heard. The neighbour who was getting ready to leave to go to work, the neighbourhood cat who looked in at the window looking for cuddles, the dogs who began barking after being awakened by the noise.

The little, yet older Nicole was stunned for a few seconds, while her father sadly continued his makeshift breakfast. Now everything was clear, mum was cheating on my father, thought Nicole. How disappointing, it isn't possible, but it seems to be the truth, the stark truth, she believes her father, he is a good man.

As soon as Nicole had the courage to pull herself together, she asked her father who the man was, the man who "stole" her mum from her family, the man who was destroying everything. To Nicole's mind, it was as if her mum had been forced to start that new relationship.

Innocently, Nicole did not understand that betrayal is the result of the will of two people, not just one.

Matías looked at her straight and told her that maybe it was better to get ready for the day ahead, by now it was morning. "Go and get ready, Nicole, you have to go, and I'll have to go to work soon, too".

"No, dad, no, I want to know who that bloody man is". Before then, Nicole would never have used words like that, she was kind and polite. "I want to know who that bloody man who is destroying, killing our family is".

Matías almost started to smile, knowing that his reply would irritate Nicole even more, and confessed. "That man is Mr Paul, your PE teacher".

Boom!!, the second bomb of that morning exploded, Nicole laughed, but a second later the laugh turned into an endless flood of heavy and very salty tears. At that point, it was all over, for Nicole life had become a nightmare from which she would never wake up again. In a matter of minutes, the certainties of a young girl had been annihilated, all that Nicole had always dreamt of for herself and her family had turned into a nasty story that was best forgotten.

Nicole now lives with her father. Her mum, for want of a better phrase, ran off with her new partner.

Nicole changed school and, together with her brother and their father, moved to another city. Their life continues, they grow up and the lesson that learnt marked her permanently. She dreams of finding love, but she is terrified of it. She never went on that trip to Istanbul.

MICHAELA

The thing I love most in a woman is her smile. When I see a woman smile, I can honestly say that my soul rejoices. It's as if the universe is telling me that the woman is happy and I think that wanting the happiness of others is the first important step to reaching one's own.

Michaela's face is the personification of happiness, purity, the joy of living in this odd, mad world, full of stress and challenges, yet she tackles them with a smile.

I want to emphasise that I'm talking about a sincere smile, never forced by the situation at hand, a smile that uses a seemingly simple gesture to express a love of life.

If I could give a gift to all the women in the world, I would give them an unmistakable, genuine smile.

However, it goes without saying, not all that glitters is gold, because behind that smile there is a different story, an incredible and sometimes cruel story.

My study and the desire to write this book is about this profound aspect in people, and specifically women, skilled chameleons, able to cleverly hide their true feelings, behind smiles or approaches, who try to cloud the eyes of those who look at them, to defend themselves, to survive.

So many stories and so much suffering hidden behind those looks, and that fascinates me. I would like to know about all their lives and, perhaps, try to help them in my own small way, clearly aware of the difficulty of the task. This book is an attempt to shine a light on their souls, to show the world that women are unique and special beings.

In this case, I want to respect this young woman's desire for her story not to be a tale of what she has been through. I will limit myself to telling you that she had to overcome two very particular moments in her young life. In the first phase, when she was still only thirteen, she fought against the onset of an illness that is unfortunately still widespread, anorexia. A few years later, she also had to deal with bulimia. Thanks to her fortitude, she managed to overcome both situations and, as she was growing up, her awareness transformed her into what she is today. Now she is a woman who is becoming increasingly mature, her experiences have made her strong and ready to face the world.

Michaela lives with her family, she's twenty-six, she's very young, full of energy and a desire to live and try things. She has a younger sister who drives her mad, but whom she loves deeply. Then there's mum and dad. Hers is a beautiful family. From an early age, Michaela has always had a dream, that of becoming an important person, able to change the world and accomplish new things, perhaps things that can improve the lives of others, as well as her own.

She has seen lots of beautiful things in her young life and dreams of achieving her primary goal: to be happy and at peace with the world. She's still very green and the experience of life will help her grow up, her story is that of a continuous search for freedom, the heavens will help her and her tenacity will make her great.

She adores animals, who she cares for and loves as one loves a person, her pure and kind soul allows her to communicate with all living things in this world, as only a candid soul can do.

I wish her a world of happiness and joy, she has the right to receive back the beauty that she gives to everyone, with her smile, with her transparency, with her sincerity, always.

Michaela lives in Detmold in Germany, and her life smiles at her, because she always smiles at life.

REFLECTING

During my trips, both for work and for recreation, I meet and have met a great many people. Normally, I manage to look inside them, even within just a few minutes of knowing them. Their stories subsequently confirm what I had already guessed and are often proof of what my instincts had already revealed to me. Ah, if I had only listened to my instinct more often, perhaps I would now be a different person, undoubtedly more mature, certainly more free. However, the road of life is paved with experiences and the search for confirmation very often obscures the truth or the very perception of reality.

I have spoken to so many people who have unconsciously "bared" their souls to me, had so many discussions without listening to their words, because their eyes already told me everything I needed to know.

My manner of talking to people has always given me the opportunity to understand them deeply. Without knowing it, I was in touch with them right away and the facts always proved that to be the case later on.

What am I talking about?

I'm talking about obvious lies, hidden by fake smiles. I'm talking about the clear contrast between what a person says and what they really think. I'm talking about "reading" a person without them saying anything, I'm talking about intuition, vision, instinct.

I spent many years in a sort of emotional paralysis, due to work and many other work related situations that have kept my brain engaged very busy, more so than my soul. A few years ago, thanks to myself, and to some friends, one in particular, I freed my instincts and I realised that they had been asking me to be released for quite a while. Now I understand that it was the only thing to do, let's say, better late than never.

In everyday life, and any time I manage to do so, I like listening to people's stories and, specifically, I love stories about women's lives, their mysteries and their innate fortitude.

Every woman has many facets, like a diamond, all however surrounded by the same unavoidable and powerful aura, they are all very tenacious and often complicated. Sometimes or, rather, often, I ask myself why women are so underestimated, why they are treated as inferior. Yes, I know, they are often a pain in the neck, but are they any less stressful than men? In their own way, men often know how to be even worse, differently, but still a pain in the neck, wouldn't you agree?

Women are often discriminated against, criticised and mistreated.

Let me cite a simple, but very practical, as well as fun, example, perhaps I can make you smile and reflect on things.

I have always wondered, "how can it be that no one is yet to understand that women's toilets have to be much bigger than those for men?".

A short while ago, during one of my travels, I stopped at a service area to have a coffee and go to the loo.

It's the same story every time, an endless queue of poor women of all ages, forced to wait up to an hour to access the tiny bathrooms, which have the same number of toilets as the ones for men, even though men also have urinals.

It's senseless and so obvious, but no one has ever thought to resolve the issue.

 I'd like to submit an official request via this book, for all service areas and all crowded public places to adopt a system to resolve this absurd, unreasonable situation. Good grief, is it so difficult?

Let's take a few male executives and force them to go to the loo sitting down, waiting an hour for their turn. I think they would gain a greater understanding of the problem at hand.

Sorry, I just had to get it off my chest, it's one of the things against the female sex that I've never understood. It would be so easy to resolve the issue. There isn't the will to do so or, perhaps, it's a lack of respect?

RUNNING AWAY

Running away from the routine every day is an important and indispensable goal for women. The stories I've told above allowed me to look inside incredible people, great women who often gave their best years to the wrong person, yet despite everything are often still involved in the lives of these undeserving exploiters. Women who sacrificed themselves for their families, for their children, for their work. Dreamers awakened from a deep sleep, convinced that it was all a joke, then realistically catapulted into the stark reality, too late, when the mess had already been made.

Nowadays, things have changed, improved, from my point of view. Women have matured and realised that perhaps it's not worth it, they are often happier because they are finally aware that a perfect life does not exist, that a perfect partner does not exist, that perfection is a concept that should not be part of anyone's life. Life should be a journey and its goal should be self-improvement. Nowadays, they aim for the sort of happiness that also has room for compromises, which leads them to a higher, deeper level.

They have undoubtedly realised that time is the most precious thing they possess and wasting it in the pursuit of perfection is a losing battle.

Inside, I dream of a future that puts women in an ideal position to allow them to achieve their desires. I dream of a world in which women consciously become the drivers of change.

Their future must no longer be tied to the dominant presence of arrogance and frustration. Their freedom must, first and foremost, commence from how they are perceived. The future is in their hands.

Let's give space and support to the female sex, let's give them the opportunity to emerge, grow and achieve happiness. Women are the mirror of all mankind and their freedom is the basis for a safer and longer lasting future. If we succeed in transforming their lives by helping them, boredom and apathy will no longer be part of their lives and their fortitude will become the vital energy that sustains us in the challenges of the coming decades.

MAKE-UP

Oscar Wilde once said: "A man's face is his autobiography. A woman's face is her work of fiction".

The term "make-up" or, in other words, deception, says as much. Yes, because the make-up that every woman in the world uses is, in my opinion, merely a deception, excuse my frankness, but that's what it is.

There is a famous saying that states that a woman is truly beautiful if, having just awoken in the morning without make-up, you still think she is. It's something I agree with, a woman in her natural state is the most beautiful creature it is possible to behold. I think all the camouflage resulting from make-up is too obvious. Especially in these last few years, in which very young girls have also begun to use this trick to look older and more "mature".

I love simple women, I respect them all, but seeing girls practically masked behind their make-up merely validates the theory that it's all about appearances, regardless of content.

Women, try this, put on less make-up, let others appreciate you for what you really are, with all your imperfections and insecurities. You don't have to stand out at all costs. You're more than the mask that you insist on wearing, every day, on all occasions, skilled beguilers. You hide behind the safety of a perfect face, which will obviously never be perfect. We are all imperfect that is precisely what makes us unique and makes every woman unique.

The continuous effort to look like famous actresses and models does nothing but increase the sense of frustration and inadequacy. Show your true self, your soul will thank you and your uniqueness will make a mark in everyone's hearts.

Nowadays, there are legions of young girls who all look the same, same haircut, same clothes, same make-up, same attitude. Where has individual personality gone?

Modern society wants us all stereotyped and enclosed in a single circle, but I'm not putting up with that. Leave the ordinary behind, young girls, refuse cosmetic surgery, it only leads to frustration. Refuse to look like this or that actress or model, be unique, be yourself, with all your strengths and, why not, your little flaws. Decide to swim against the tide and make sure that's your guiding light.

Even you women who are no longer young, evidently driven to use these tricks to improve your image of always impeccable and pleasant ladies, reject the need to stand out at all costs. The passing years are the mirror of your soul, covering it in colours and tints will only suffocate it, the soul doesn't need make-up in order to stand out.

Happiness and freedom live elsewhere, they certainly don't reside in the brush of your eyeshadows or at the tip of your brightest lipstick.

I can already hear the murmur of many female readers. It's you men who want us to perfect, it is your fault if we have to look like the much vaunted models and actresses. We're competing because of you, that is what forces us to resemble your perception of the ideal woman!

This is undoubtedly partly true, but you women are unique beings and your uniqueness will never be enhanced by the type of make-up you use, it only serves to deceive the absent-minded passer-by.

I realise my statements may offend some of you and I duly apologise, far be it from me to wish to do so, but I sincerely urge you to try and take a step back, even if it's not in your nature, given how combative you are. Try to show yourselves as you are, natural, without exaggerations, without excesses. The road to your freedom will open wide.

I love women who are free, transparent women, women who are simply unique.

BRIDES

How many television programmes are based on stories of future brides in search of happiness? I think there must be dozens of reality shows that each day try to capture the life and despair of young brides to be, who would do anything to have the best wedding ever. Everything starts with the search for a location, the choice of wedding dress, the shoes, everything has to be perfect, because it has to be the wedding of the year. The preparations turn into a stressful and unnerving journey to the fateful "I do".

Long gone are the times when a marriage was truly a symbol of love and fidelity, when the ceremony and the preparations observed time-honoured rites and traditions. Nowadays, the future groom no longer sends months and months courting his bride to be. The future groom would ask the bride's father for her hand and it all depended on his decision, which was almost always affirmative, but deeply thought over.

Nowadays, everything has turned into a race to stand out, as if the promise of marriage were only a tenth part of the marriage, in terms of importance.

The choice of the wedding dress and all the accessories take months of healthy emotional preparation for the ceremony. Everything becomes secondary and the event turns into a nerve-racking challenge.

I hate this approach to weddings. I love simple things, but above all, I love knowing that some of you aren't looking for happiness in material things. You're seeking pleasure in all the other moments you have spent and will spend together with your partner and that's the most important thing.

Television programmes depict life as if it were a competition, to drive us towards looking for the best of everything, but the best of everything are you women and the love you can give, regardless of the colour of the wedding dress, the type of shoes and the menu at the reception. You are the only thing that matters, everything else is just the trimming and is not important.

Focus your care and attention only on your feelings and your heart, everything else will sort itself out.

TEARS

When I think of the sea and perhaps women, too, a strange picture often pops into my head. I try to quantify how many tears women all over the world have shed. Why do I place tears and women together? Because they are the only ones able to cry when they need to. It is believed that women also live longer because of that, too.

I don't know if that's true, but I think it's probable.

Have you ever seen a man cry? Perhaps only in films.

Tears are often a liberation and, when they are shed due to sadness or mourning, they seem to act like a medicine. Bitter tears, seeking to purify the blurred stares of a sombre moment.

Obviously, being an optimist, I love tears of joy, tears that flow abundantly from a healthy laugh and, in my opinion, flow so abundantly because they include those that were not shed in times of deep emotion and sadness.

How many times have you been ashamed to let go and cry in front of someone? Why is crying seen as a weakness? How much of your life has been spent keeping back your emotions and your tears?

Nowadays it seems that the best show of strength is never letting allowing your emotions to take over. It appears to have become standard behaviour.

However, your emotions will allow you to survive the attempt to make us all the same, without feelings, without heart, without emotions. Emotion is a luxury that they don't want us to enjoy, let's take back this luxury.

Other people's freedom and "folly" are often seen as a disease, but what is a bit of healthy folly, after all?

It is the manner that many have adopted in order to face the world, before everyone. It is the desire to express oneself without filters, it is the ability of a few to feel free to laugh, cry and play, even as adults.

If there is someone close to you who suffocates these emotions, perhaps you should avoid them, your freedom is more important.

Tears are like steam inside a pressure cooker, at a certain point you have to let it out. Your heart and your soul will thank you.

87

MUMS

It would probably need a whole book, just to talk about them, mothers, these mysterious beings that are unknown to many.

The word "mum" comes from a simplification of the word "mother", which is one of the first words that children say when they learn to speak, it starts as "ma-ma" and turns into "mum".

While I say that women are strong, it can certainly be said that a mum is a woman elevated to the Nth degree. Incredibly always present, attentive to every slight nuance, capable of inhuman efforts and a powerful glue that keeps families together. In years gone by, perhaps they were more present or perhaps now they are present in a different way. In the past, mums were often forced to remain silent for the good name of the family, divorces were rarer and women who were mums were forced to stifle their anger in order to protect their children and the image of the happy family. Nowadays, everything has become simpler, we get married and get divorced with a click of the fingers, it's "almost" strange to have had only one husband or not to be divorced or separated for some reason or other. The cause of this ease with which we change partners may be due to progress, modernity or maybe the fault of WhatsApp.

However, even in these modern times, a mum is still a mum. Able to solve any problem, skilled in simultaneously managing children, grandchildren, a husband and all family crises that afflict their lives on a daily basis, in sickness and in health. Mums that are desperate and always misunderstood, mums that are often alone, who keep each other company to compare notes and try to survive.

Was it easier to be a mum forty years ago? Perhaps.

Perhaps once, when mobile phones, internet and Facebook did not exist, managing children was simpler and the dangers of cyber space did not exist. Today's mums are not quite capable of controlling the explosion of social media, the web and everything that lies behind the screen of a mobile phone or a computer. Besides having to fight the traditional fight against known dangers, nowadays they have to arm themselves to fight a new enemy, called the web.

I love mums and I try to understand where all their energy, both physical and emotional, comes from. An advertisement that makes me smile is the one in which a man is in bed with a minor cold and, with the look of someone who is on his last legs, says to his wife: "call my mother...", clearly insinuating that he might not make it through the night.

That line never fails to make me laugh, but at the same time also causes me a little emotion, you could almost say that it moves me, because an amusing advertisement manages to contain the essence of what a mum represents.

"Call my mother" can, in my opinion, be translated as "I want to live". Call the only person who is so strong that she can save my life. A man who asks a woman to call another woman, in this case his mum, to save him. Epic, I would say.

It is a very personal interpretation, but it contains the meaning of the female figure of a mum.

After all, it's a unique and irreplaceable figure, a mum is forever, both for sons and daughters, our mum protects us, cares for us, is constantly worried about us, whether we are three or forty years of age. Mum is a woman who has created a new life. Only she has pre-emptive rights on that life.

Only she knows the suffering of having given birth to a new human being. Only she is emotionally authorised to demand respect from her children, she alone.

Long live women who are mothers, they are quite simply unique.

HYSTERIA

Every time we hear this word, we tend to make specific reference to women, for some reason, because it seems that only women can be hysterical, which often appears true, but is not an absolute.

Let's forget all the scientific explanations of the state of hysteria, whether male or female, for a moment. Men are also often hysterical, but when that happens they are labelled "stressed".

All told, female hysteria is nothing but an accumulation of great stress, both emotional and existential, which is superficially defined as a kind of madness that "only", it seems, affects women.

On this point, I would like to emphasise that we all live in various stages of our existence, moments that are more or less euphoric, more or less stressful, more or less hysterical. Associating hysteria exclusively to the female half of mankind is now a thing of the past.

Try to put yourself in the shoes of a mother, a woman with a job or a woman with children, etc. The mere fact of being a woman continually tests their tenacity and their ability to resist pressure, criticism, the mere fact of always having to look perfect, at all times, anywhere. Men tend to use the word hysteria to describe a whole series of symptoms that women manifest, believing that the word itself was coined specifically for the female sex. This approach is at the very least offensive and derogatory. Telling a woman that she's hysterical is like telling a man he's mad, not in the positive sense of being eccentric, but mad like someone who is wrong in the head. I would say that it's extremely offensive, wouldn't you agree?

Receiving this "compliment" whenever a woman is feeling the stress or pressure must be very disheartening. I can honestly say that I have never told a woman that she was hysterical, at most I may have said that she was nervous or angry, which can happen to anyone.

Let's try to call states of mind by their appropriate names, for respect towards these unique creatures and ourselves. Words have their dose of importance. Passing hasty judgments, without weighing the terms used, will only lead to trouble.

If we men could put ourselves in a woman's shoes of a woman, I don't think we would want to stay in them for much, which is the truth of it. Female hysteria does not exist, there is only a highly pronounced state of stress that women, who are emotionally more sensitive, tend to manifest more vehemently, that's all.

WOMEN

The origin of the word "donna" ("woman") is very interesting, it comes from the Latin domina, the feminine of dominus, i.e. lady, proprietor.

Therefore, the definition of the word "woman" contains everything I have tried to convey in this book. A woman is an owner, yes, the proprietor of the world, the only representative of the future of mankind. Women of every kind and race, but all united by the same universal ability to transform nothing into everything.

Women who transform themselves and seek happiness, often in material things, by standing out or emulating their kind, sadly influenced by the power of television and glossy magazines. Women who are unaware that the most beautiful being they can represent is reflected every morning in the mirror which reflects their own image. Without hypocrisy, without exaggeration, full of the light that only their eyes can give off.

 I would like a world in which you women feel unique all the times. Just for yourselves. Without having to prove anything to anyone, without superstructures, without needing to look like anyone else. You are unique thanks to what you represent, that's the only thing that matters, everything else is just a lot of hot air.

I dream of a world in which women can recapture their true identity. Be the only representatives of a mysterious and ancestral force. Be the only beings able to transform life into something unique and unrepeatable.

Let's save ourselves from fear and insecurity, let's give women the power to be truly free, the universe will judge us favourably.

Dedicated with affection to all women, splendid creatures that you are.

ABOUT THE AUTHOR

Matthew Calber was born in New York on 28 October 1973. The son of merchants of Italian descent, he spent his life in the Big Apple and England, where he works on behalf of the family. During his travels, he has visited many cities in Europe and America, in which he has met many people. At forty-three years of age, he has decided to write this book, a tale of true stories of women he has met and with whom he has built good friendships. It is a transparent and touching account, of how women's lives are filled with emotions and contrasting moods.

A sincere book, written with the heart and with the desire to look inside the soul of every woman.

www.ingramcontent.com/pod-product-compliance
Lightning Source LLC
Chambersburg PA
CBHW051231160726
47994CB00002B/836